GH00888749

What Christians
Should Know About...

The Importance
of Forgiveness

John Arnott

Sovereign World

ISBN: 1 85240 215 6

Scripture quotations are taken from the HOLY BIBLE, NEW INTERNATIONAL
VERSION. Copyright © 1973, 1978, 1984 by International Bible Society.
Used by permission.

This Sovereign World book is distributed in North America by Renew Books,
a ministry of Gospel Light, Ventura, California, USA. For a free catalog of resources
from Renew Books/Gospel Light, please contact your Christian supplier
or call 1-800-4-GOSPEL.

SOVEREIGN WORLD LIMITED
P.O. Box 777, Tonbridge, Kent TN11 0ZS, England.

Printed in the UK by Sussex Litho Ltd, Chichester, West Sussex.

Contents

1   Mercy Triumphs Over Justice   5

2   Choosing to Forgive   17

3   Set Free From the Fruits of Judgement   27
    (Carol Arnott)

4   It's Time to Forgive   33

About the Author

An international speaker and teacher, John Arnott is known for his ministry of renewal.

His home is Toronto, Ontario, Canada where he was born and raised, and where he now fills the position of Senior Pastor of Toronto Airport Christian Fellowship. While pastoring in Ontario, John has co-ordinated many new church plants.

John attended Ontario Bible College. He then pursued a varied and successful career in business. In 1980, while on a ministry trip to Indonesia, John responded to God's call on his life for full-time ministry.

He and his wife, Carol, planted their first church, Jubilee Christian Fellowship, of Stratford, Ontario, in 1981. They then started the Toronto church in 1988.

Experience as a businessman, husband, father and pastor, has given John a rich, blended ministry of God's grace, healing and deliverance. But he puts special emphasis on the Father heart of God, which has impacted many people with God's life-changing love and grace.

Since January 20, 1994, John and Carol have invested much time and energy into imparting God's anointing to people in many different cities and nations. They are welcomed and loved wherever they go.

1

Mercy Triumphs Over Justice

Forgiveness is a key to blessing. Forgiveness and repentance open up our hearts and allow the river of God to flow freely in us. We need to give the Holy Spirit permission to bring to our minds those things that need to be resolved in our hearts.

Three things are vital to seeing a powerful release of the Spirit of God in our own lives and in the world around us.

First, we need a revelation of how big God is. We must know that absolutely nothing is impossible for Him (Luke 1:37). Second, we need a revelation of how loving He is, how much He cares for us and how He is absolutely committed to loving us to life (Jeremiah 31:3). I delight to tell people that God loves them just the way they are, yet loves them too much to leave them the way they are.

Finally, we need a revelation of how we can walk in that love and give it away. A heart that is free has time and resources for others.

Energy Draining Wounds

I have pastored for over seventeen years. One thing I have discovered is that woundedness and devastation in people's hearts and lives saps much of their energy and resources. People expend so much energy on simply trying to make it through another day, that there is little left over to give away to others.

When we ask people about believing God for things like missions, for giving offerings or receiving miracles, many say, "I can hardly see my way clear to reach tomorrow, let alone really go for God with abandonment." The key for us, I believe, is locked up in the whole issue of repentance and forgiveness.

I believe God has us prophetically at the place of the threshing floor. The Lord is breaking off that hard outer shell and preparing us to become "food" for the nations. When the wheat is separated from the chaff, then the wheat is ready to use.

People asked John the Baptist if he was the Messiah, and he answered them,

> *I baptize you with water. But one more powerful than I will come, the thongs of whose sandals I am not worthy to untie. He will baptize you with the Holy Spirit and with fire.*
>
> (Luke 3:16)

Don't we love that scripture? How many messages have you heard on receiving the Holy Spirit lately? But let's read the next verse.

> *His winnowing fork is in his hand to clear his threshing floor and to gather the wheat into his barn, but he will burn up the chaff with unquenchable fire.* (v. 17)

The Lord is telling us, right on the front end of our commitment to Him, that He is committed to burning up the chaff in our lives. Are you willing to have Him do that? Are you sure?

> *"Love the Lord your God with all your heart and with all your soul and with all your mind." This is the first and greatest commandment. And the second is like it: "Love your neighbour as yourself."* (Matthew 22:37-39)

Many prophetic words are now going forth regarding missions and evangelism. I believe the Lord told me that the first missionaries went out because they were scattered by persecution. But the missionaries and evangelists He is sending out now are going because they are scattered by the absolute love of God.

It is God's love that is hooking us, constraining us and drawing us with a motive that is pure and right before the Lord. We want to go out loving and serving, and see this great harvest come in, the harvest of the end times. With this demanding mandate from the Lord, we have no energy to spare trying to keep a lid on personal problems and issues.

Critical Thoughts and Words

Negative things in our lives can block us from going out in love to serve others. Our thoughts and our words can hinder us from moving freely in the grace of Christ. Paul spoke of the importance of this:

> *The weapons we fight with are not the weapons of the world. On the contrary, they have divine power to demolish strongholds. We demolish arguments and every pretension that sets itself up against the knowledge of God, and we take captive every thought to make it obedient to Christ.*
>
> (2 Corinthians 10:5)

Some years ago we offered a course called "Pure in Heart," written by Mark Virkler from Buffalo, New York. This course was worth a million dollars to me. It moved the issues of life from the theoretical and theological right down into the heart.

I will never forget the second chapter, "Discerning the Accuser from the Comforter." In it, Mark made this outrageous statement that every negative thing and thought is always of the enemy, and every positive, life-giving, up-building thought is always of the Holy Spirit. He said the enemy is always negative, and the Holy Spirit is always positive.

Since I was just learning in those days how to hear the voice of the Lord, I didn't realize that God would often speak in our thoughts. I believed that if we would be diligent in prayer, press in and fast, then maybe once a long while we would hear His voice. The drapes might blow, thunder would crash; it would be spectacular. Then we would say, "God spoke to me today."

I didn't know, however, that He spoke through ordinary thoughts. It had never occurred to me that there was and is a still small voice behind me saying, *"This is the way; walk in it"* (Isaiah 30:21).

As we learned that the Lord spoke in this way, it didn't come as too big a shock to realize that the devil spoke that way too. You can easily hear the devil talking to you. Have you ever heard him whispering in your ear? Yet God, who is much more powerful, is speaking to you all the time as well.

Mark went on to develop this whole theme. The accuser accuses, and the Comforter comforts. Simple, yet profound.

Mark had discovered in his own heart and life as a believer that approximately 80 percent of his thinking was negative, critical and accusatory, and only 20 percent was positive. Eighty percent negative!

To reinforce these statistics, he had little tests for us to take. Not only did the class results confirm the 80 percent critical thinking, but 80 percent of my own thinking was negative as well. It so smote me in my heart. I prayed, "God, this is completely unacceptable—completely! I cannot go through my life with 80 percent of my mind yielded to the enemy, to the accuser!" How about you?

When you listen in on Christian conversations and listen to the world's conversations, you find that others have the same problem. What do people talk about? They discuss their injustices. They rehearse what other people have done to them or against them. They go on about how they have been hurt. They bring a rationale as to why they were innocent victims and others were guilty of hurting and mistreating them.

So, we are in this predicament where 80 percent of the time our thoughts are yielded to negative and judgmental thinking – thoughts that are really of the enemy. And we wonder why in the world we are not enjoying more of the blessings of God!

I remember responding, "Oh, God, You know I need You to help me with this one. I need You to give me a jab every time my mind starts to be negative and critical about people because I don't want to do this, Lord." I knew I didn't have the resources and the self-discipline to get on top of it. I was afraid to promise Him that I would stop. I needed a miracle that would transform my heart and thinking, so my thoughts could be positive and life-giving.

Choosing to Speak Life

In Genesis 3 we find the story about two unique trees in the Garden of Eden. I have taught about them for years. Rick Joyner has written about them, and so has Ted Haggard in his book Primary Purpose.

In the Garden grew two trees; the tree of life and the tree of the knowledge of good and evil. Which one did Adam and Eve eat of? Of course, they chose the tree of the knowledge of good and evil. Why? They were tempted, wanting to be like God, knowing good and evil.

We could call this tree "the tree of judgment." In our pride and self-sufficiency we think we have enough understanding and information to make fair and honest judgments in every situation. We instinctively judge much of the time, and when we judge, we are usually negative, biased and unfair.

I believe the Holy Spirit is calling us to turn away from judging. We need to refrain from judging situations and judging one another, and instead bless and forgive so that life will flow.

Ted Haggard states that when we partake of the tree of the knowledge of good and evil, that is, the tree of judgment – it always produces accusation. When we accuse, we come into agreement with Satan, the accuser of the brethren. It is either someone else's fault or your own fault, but somebody is always to blame when accusations fly. Isn't that right? That is the human condition. Our constant judging of others causes us to be negative, negative, negative. A continual cry for justice is always being raised up to God.

Now that you and I have been born again and filled with the Holy Spirit, the tree of life has been put back into the gardens of our hearts. If we will eat of the tree of life, what will happen? It will build us up, encourage us, and edify us and others. The tree of life will give life to others as we bless and curse not, forgive and accuse not.

I was with Pastor John Kilpatrick of the Brownsville Assembly of God in Pensacola, Florida, in May 1996. He described to me how years ago, he had spent much time in prayer over his church's need for music ministry. He had often prayed, "Oh God, I want an orchestra."

He would walk through the empty orchestra area. He had nobody to play any instruments, only the piano. Day after day he would complain about the emptiness. He would ask the Lord where the people were. "What is wrong with the body of Christ? Why don't they serve? Why don't they get in here and play?" He was cursing the whole thing with his words of judgment and condemnation.

One day the Lord spoke to him, "John, why don't you bless them instead?" The concept shocked him, but he began to walk through the place and say, "Lord, I bless this whole orchestra pit. I bless the people you are going to send. Lord, let the favor of God come upon them. I bless their hearts to want to play and worship and serve the King of kings and Lord of lords."

It wasn't too long before someone came to him and said, "You know, I have a trumpet and I used to play a little bit. I'm not all that good, but I'd like to play along with the piano, if that is all right." John was taken aback, but he said, "Great! Come on." And the next thing he knew, one after another, they came. The whole orchestra area filled up with musicians.

Most important, God taught him the value of blessing and speaking words of life. The rest is history with the mighty revival that has occurred at his church.

It is so important to speak life and not death.

Remember the saying, "It is better to light one little candle than it is to curse the darkness?" Isn't that good? We have to do something to bring our own thoughts into captivity. We must desire to change. My prayer is, "Lord, I would like the numbers to be completely reversed. At the very least, help me to be only 20 percent negative and 80 percent positive." That would be more like it. How about for you?

Settle this issue in your heart. The Holy Spirit is always positive, and Satan is always negative. That sounded extreme to me at first. I had to process and cross-examine that for several weeks before I finally agreed it was true. I concluded that even when God brings correction, it is always in a positive direction and His intent is always life-giving and redemptive. That is His heart.

The enemy, on the other hand, is always negative. *"The thief comes only to steal and kill and destroy"* (John 10:10). He is always the accuser, the destroyer. His intent is to bring guilt, fear, hopelessness, sin and accusation. If we want to bring our thoughts into subjection and captivity, we need to get free of the holds the enemy has upon our lives (2 Corinthians 10:5).

Ted Haggard declares that partaking of the tree of life – allowing the Holy Spirit to fill us and flow through us, and blessing and forgiving those around us – will always produce innocence. Where there is no accusation, there is no guilt.

Adam and Eve were innocent in the garden before they ate of the tree of the knowledge of good and evil. Haggard notes that the anointing of the Holy Spirit will only flow through innocence. That shocked me, but I knew it was truth.

We don't get ensnared so much in talking about people we are not close to, such as the man down the street or the woman in the next town. People we don't have close relationships with don't usually hurt us or anger us deeply.

But the ones who can upset us are those we are close to – husbands, wives, parents, primary authority figures, pastors, teachers, employers, friends and those we have high expectations of. These people have the potential to hurt us. Because of that, we can get into a pattern of judging them and thinking wrong thoughts about them which, in turn, produces accusation.

The Law of Judgment

The Holy Spirit desires to search and work deep in our own hearts.

> *Do not judge, or you too will be judged. For in the same way you judge others, you will be judged, and with the measure you use, it will be measured to you.* (Matthew 7:1-2)

Do you believe that scripture? Jesus said it, I believe it, that settles it – right? What He is saying here is that if you demand justice and repayment for sins and wrongs done to you, then you will be dealt with according to your own prescription. The way you treat people is the way you will be treated.

When I understood this dynamic, I thought, Lord, I want to be the most forgiving, loving and understanding person on the face of the earth. I don't want to get what I deserve – not from God, not from Satan and not from life.

The Lord spoke to me years ago about this principle in Scripture: Justice is good, but mercy is better. Justice is the law of

God. It means that if you hurt me, I can hurt you. If you wrong someone, then that wrong must be made right. Our sense of justice understands this. An eye for an eye, a tooth for a tooth, a life for a life. Very, very fair.

If you want justice, then you will be dealt with by the same rules. It is the Law of God, and it is good and fair, but it is also the arena in which Satan really shines. He is the master prosecutor, the master accuser. The problem is, none of us could ever have any hope for eternity if we all received the justice we deserved. There is, however, a place to go where Satan cannot follow and accuse. That place is the grace of the Lord Jesus Christ. The place of mercy, love and forgiveness.

It is a higher and better place. If we live in grace and mercy, Satan cannot follow us there. He has no rights there. Did you know that? But if you spend 80 percent of your time on the judgment/justice level, then he has the right to beat you 80 percent of the time. My cry is, "God, help me to live more in the grace of God."

> *Why do you look at the speck of sawdust in your brother's eye and pay no attention to the plank in your own eye? How can you say to your brother, "Let me take the speck out of your eye," when all the time there is a plank in your own eye? You hypocrite, first take the plank out of your own eye, and then you will see clearly to remove the speck from your brother's eye.* (Matthew 7:3-5)

It seems we have X-Ray vision to see the shortcomings of others, yet seem quite blind to our own. Understanding this is a major key to freedom. Jesus is saying judge yourself first. When you want mercy for your own sins, then you tend to go much easier on others. Begin to bless and curse not. It will bring you tremendous release.

Much energy is expended in keeping our angers, hurts and fears pushed down. We are often not even in touch with those things in ourselves. But as we live in mercy and grace, releasing and forgiving others from these issues, we will find His yoke is easy and His burden is light (Matthew 12:30).

The Law of Sowing and Reaping

Let's hear the words of our Lord,

> *Do not judge, and you will not be judged. Do not condemn, and you will not be condemned. Forgive, and you will be forgiven. Give, and it will be given to you. A good measure, pressed down, shaken together and running over, will be poured into your lap. For with the measure you use, it will be measured to you.*

> (Luke 6:37-38)

Isn't it amazing how often we view this sowing and reaping dynamic only in terms of giving and financial blessing? Yet this is not merely speaking of finances, it is across the board. It is for releasing the incredible grace of God.

In Exodus 20:4 we are told that the sins of the fathers are visited upon the children to the third and the fourth generation. As we see recurring patterns of negative things happening to us, we can also see how the enemy has had access and inroads into our lives. He wants to maintain those inroads right down through the family line for several generations.

Consider, for example, an alcoholic father who in turn has an alcoholic son who in turn has an alcoholic son. Or a young lady who grows up in an alcoholic home and vows to herself, "I will never marry a man who is an alcoholic."

Five years after the wedding she is saying, "I can't stand living with him anymore. He is an alcoholic; he is beating me; he is mean to the children. He is just like my father." And we say, "Dear God, what is wrong with people's heads? Couldn't they see this coming?"

An incredible "magnetic pull" draws people so they play into the hands of the enemy. It is the law of God's justice, and Satan is a master legalist. He takes advantage of the law of sowing and reaping (Galatians 6:7-8). People make judgments toward their parents, judgments which give the enemy the legal right to perpetuate the crime. Yet the heart of God is to forgive and heal.

Justice Or Mercy?

Jesus took what we deserve upon Himself, on the cross. When you or I say, "I hate my alcoholic father;" when we (rightly) accuse and blame him for things he has done and said; we are really crying for justice. We are making a judgment that is rooted in hurt and bitterness. When we demand justice, we are actually stepping back into a legal system that has power to demand justice and payment for our sins as well. It is like giving the devil a key to your house.

The only safe response is, "Lord, let there be mercy. Let mercy triumph over judgment (James 2:13). You have forgiven me all this great debt of mine. Now that you have given me the keys to the kingdom, I am going to forgive everybody who owes me anything or has hurt me in any way."

Remember the story recorded in Matthew 18:23-35 in which Jesus told about the great king who loaned money to one of his servants. The man ran up a debt of millions of dollars.

One day the king called him in and demanded, "Pay back what you owe me." The man said, "I can't. Have mercy on me and give me time and I will pay you back everything." But the King said, "No. I want it now. Sell him. Sell his family. Liquidate everything he has. We will recover as much as we can."

So the man fell down and begged for forgiveness, saying, "Please have mercy upon me." So the king said, "Okay, you'll never be able to pay the debt back anyway, so forget it. Just go on about your business. I release you from the debt." How relieved and thankful that man must have been.

Soon after that, however, Jesus describes how that same man went out and took his fellow servant by the neck, saying, "Pay me the 50 dollars you owe me!" His fellow servant replied with the same story. "Have mercy on me. Give me time and I will pay you all of it back." But he said, "No way!" and had him thrown in jail until the debt was paid.

The word got back to the king. He called the man in and he said, "You wicked servant. I had compassion and mercy upon you for this huge debt that you owed me. Could you not have had mercy upon your fellow servant?"

Even though I knew that story, I was tempted to rationalize that I didn't sin that badly compared to everybody else. A dualism was going on in my heart – I wanted mercy for myself, but justice in my dealings with others. "They hurt me, they said this, they did that, they owe me and I want it put right." But for myself, I wanted grace and mercy.

We can't have it both ways. If I am going to say I want justice because someone hurt me, then I cannot ask for mercy for myself. That is what the wicked manager did. But if I try to exact justice, I have fallen from the place of grace and mercy, back to what is fair.

The truth is, people hurt people. Parents hurt their children. Children hurt their parents. Many people have been hurt by pastors. Many pastors have been hurt by their people. This is happening all over in the body of Christ. We ask people, "What was your father like? What was your mother like? How about your older brothers, how did they respond to you?" We often find years of baggage and judgments that people, for the most part, are not in touch with. Then they wonder why recurring patterns of pain and rejection are in their lives.

I have talked to people who have had three or four auto accidents in a row and who think, What's going on? Do I wear a sign that says, "Hit me"? No, a dynamic of sowing and reaping is taking place.

The Lord says that the sins of the fathers will be visited on the children. (Ex 20:5) This is a law of God – a law of justice, a law of sowing and reaping. Satan will see to it that this law of God is fulfilled when he can use it to destroy. Therefore the same issue or a similar issue comes to your door again. The only place of escape and safety is in the mercy and grace of the Lord Jesus Christ.

The Place of Mercy

Why not come to the place where we say, "Lord I forgive everybody of everything," and we let go of and lay down our claims for justice and repayment. The injustices are laid at the cross, and the

15

mercy and grace of Christ can then flow into our lives. Love then covers a multitude of sins (1 Peter 4:8).

The kingdom of God is not about keeping religious rules and regulations; it is about righteousness, peace and joy in the Holy Spirit (Romans 14:17). That joy is something you and I have as we live and remain in the place of mercy.

2

Choosing to Forgive

Aren't these wonderful days? God is blessing so abundantly. I see many people forgiving each other and repenting to one another. As they do, they are released into great freedom; freedom to fulfill their destiny in God's kingdom.

Freed Through Forgiveness

When Carol and I started our first church in Stratford Ontario, Canada (Carol's home town of about 27,000 where everyone knows one another), we were called a cult and various other names by some of the other churches. We were the new kid in town. About twelve years later, I had the privilege of being asked to talk to a group of pastors near Toronto at one of their district meetings.

A pastor came up to me and said, "John, I need to ask your forgiveness because I was so wrong. I thought we had some kind of a corner on the kingdom of God. I believed that if it wasn't happening with us, it just wasn't worth happening. I am so sorry, and I want to ask your forgiveness." This man was formerly the pastor of a church in Stratford who had denounced us from his pulpit.

When I related this to a former member of his church, a man who was now with us in Toronto, he broke down and wept as the Lord poured His healing into that situation.

Recently a pastor from one of the largest churches in Toronto made an appointment to see me. He said, "John, I've come to ask your forgiveness." I asked him why, and he said, "I have said nasty, terrible things about you and about your church and, more important, about this move of the Spirit."

He told me that when I had originally called him up and invited him to our church because God was visiting us, he had reacted negatively and didn't want anything to do with us. He had denounced the move of God over and over again. Later he heard about revival in Pensacola, Florida, and he traveled all the way there to experience it. God so touched his heart and convicted him that now he had come to see me.

He was so moved that he also came to our Sunday morning service, which is for our congregation, and asked their forgiveness for speaking against them and the move of God. He confided, "John, we so desperately need revival. I know I have grieved the Holy Spirit by criticizing you, and I don't want any outstanding debts in the heavenlies. I don't want God to have any issues with me. I want revival for my soul and revival for my church. I want God's blessing to open up." Needless to say, a great healing came between our two churches.

Do you wonder why situations like this are being healed? God is calling His whole church into this place of repentance and forgiveness. The heavens are being torn open because people are finding out that mercy triumphs over judgment. They are willing to do what Jesus said: forgive one another, give grace to one another and love one another. We want to see forgiveness flowing for individuals, families, churches, cities and nations.

James 3 reminds us that the tongue is very powerful. Small things like the tongue can have great influence. A horse can be turned with a little bridle and a ship can be steered with a tiny rudder. Our out-of-control tongues are like deadly poison. We can say things that are to some degree irreparable. People have been deeply wounded by words spoken against them. I pray, "Oh God, oh God, put a guard over my mouth. Put a guard over my thoughts. I don't want to wound and offend."

I don't want the Holy Spirit to have those kind of issues with me. One of the most grievous things to the heart of God is all of the criticism that goes on in the lives of Christians. Nothing stops revival like criticism. God is calling us into a place of victory, a place where mercy triumphs over judgment. Remember the great debt that you owed, which was lovingly paid in full by Jesus Christ.

Our Debt to Jesus Christ

Think about the greatest crime that ever occurred among humanity, the greatest atrocity of all. It was not Hitler, Stalin, or any other despot guilty of murdering millions of people. The greatest tragedy, the greatest crime ever committed by humanity, was when our ancestors, Jews and Romans, murdered the Son of God on a rugged cross two thousand years ago.

Consider who Jesus really was. He was not just a good man. He was God the Son who came to the earth where He healed, taught, blessed, gave and shared of Himself. Wicked hands nailed Him to a cross, mocking Him for six hours while He bled to death. He endured it because there had to be an atoning payment for our sins, and the innocent paid the debts of the guilty.

It is your debt and mine that He has paid. It was our sin – yours and mine – that necessitated His execution. We are responsible for the death of God's Son. Our sins required His death, and we are the children of those who murdered Him. Most of us would have at least a drop or two of either Jewish or Roman blood.

To that debt, we have added our own lives of immorality, our pornographic secret sins and adulterous relationships, our stealing and lying and killing and backbiting. We have piled upon it our slanderous, accusing tongues and our own bitter judgments against ourselves and others.

So we had a huge, accumulated debt. Then we came to Jesus saying, "Lord, I want to settle this thing out of court. I don't want to wait until judgment day and get what I deserve. I owe you a great debt, and I am unable to pay you. Will you please have mercy on me and forgive me?" And He said, "My son, My daughter, step up into the grace and mercy of the Lord Jesus Christ. My Son took your place, your debt is paid."

Such sweet forgiveness came. It was just as though we had never sinned. Completely covered. Jesus died instead of us and paid off every debt that you and I would ever owe. It was the greatest overpayment in the history of the universe. The Son of God traded His perfect and innocent life for the guilty. God the Son Himself, paid off what you owe and what I owe. No one barely makes it into heaven; we are either in by a mile or we miss it by a mile.

God then says, "Now, if you want to live in this place where you receive my full forgiveness, you must be forgiving." That is the deal. In other words, I cannot ask for mercy for me and justice for you. It is all or nothing. It is mercy without justice, or justice without mercy. Can you see that clearly? You can have mercy or you can have justice, but you can't have both.

Choose to Forgive

*Our Father in heaven, hallowed be your name, your kingdom come, your will be done on earth as it is in heaven. Give us today our daily bread. Forgive us our debts, **as we also have forgiven** our debtors. And lead us not into temptation, but deliver us from the evil one.*

(Matthew 6:9-13, emphasis added)

Have you noticed that in there before? Forgive us "as we also have forgiven." The same way we forgive, Lord, You forgive us.

Notice particularly what Jesus goes on to say,

For if you forgive men when they sin against you, your heavenly Father will also forgive you. But if you do not forgive men their sins, your Father will not forgive your sins.

(vv. 14-15)

The choice is clear: mercy or justice. Which would you prefer? Do you want mercy?

Now, before you get paranoid and fearful, keep in mind that the grace of God has been given to help you live this out. I believe very much that it is a process. But I also believe so much hurt, fear and pain has come upon the body of Christ that it makes the process difficult. Sometimes the pain is so severe that we feel entitled to hold on to our hurt and anger.

The Trap of Self-Justification

Matthew 5:21 tells us that when we come and bring our gifts before the Lord, and there we remember that our brother has something against us, we should first go and be reconciled with him and then return and offer our gifts. Then we will have clean hearts.

Jesus tells us about the Pharisee and the publican (or tax collector). The Pharisee said, "Thank you, Lord, that I am not like that other man. I fast and I pray and I give. I do all these good things for you."

The publican came in abject humility and prayed, "Lord, be merciful to me a sinner," not comparing himself to anyone else, just admitting how guilty he was (see Luke 18:10). The Lord said that the man who came in humility went away justified, but the self-righteous one did not.

Let me bring this down to a practical level. I was in Winnipeg, Canada, preaching on the grace of God and the power of forgiveness. A man came up to me after the service shaking and very troubled. He said, "John, you don't understand what has happened to me." I listened as he told his story.

"My own father severely abused my three-year-old baby girl. A government agency became involved, and it has devastated our family. Our little girl now has nightmares all the time. Furthermore, my father denies it. My whole family is angry with me. It is an absolute tragedy, and now you are telling me I have to forgive him."

I said, "Sir, I am not telling you that you have to forgive him. I am telling you that the only way out of your prison is forgiveness, and then repentance for judging. You can have justice if you want, but if you do, realize that the enemy will see to it that you also get what you deserve. If you can work through the issues and become willing to forgive, God will give you grace and help as you unravel all this pain. Then you can remain in the place of His mercy and grace."

Some people have had unbelievable tragedies happen to them in their lives. They realize that they were the victims. They don't understand that their own recurring problems have anything to do with their sins of judging. That is what is so beguiling.

When people sin, they sin against someone else usually. Others are hurt because of it. It's not fair, is it? We may ask, "Why does God allow that?" Well, He allows it because He has given us free will. We are allowed to make right choices or wrong choices. We may choose to love or we may choose to sin. Free will is fundamental to love. In order to have love flowing, people must be free to choose. They may choose to be near one another and bless one another, but it is of their own free will. Otherwise, we are just robots.

So we can choose to bless or we can choose to hurt (selfishness and sin). We can give life or we can give death. That choice is the responsibility that goes along with free will. Every time somebody makes a wrong choice or does something outside of love, it injures either himself or someone else—or both. Then we have what I like to call the "sinnor" (the one who has sinned) and the "sinnee" (the one who has been sinned against).

When we are the "sinnor", and the Holy Spirit reminds us of it, we want mercy, don't we? But when we are the "sinnee", we cry for justice and often become bitter. We don't realize this as a subtle trap of the enemy. If Satan can hook us through this; if he can get us demanding justice, then he will be legally entitled to bring into our lives all the reaping and punishment that we deserve.

That is the enemy's plan. That is what gives him power and legal rights. Yet Jesus, against whom the greatest crime of all was committed, didn't say, "Father, get these murderers and give them what they deserve." What was the last cry that came from his lips? *"Father, forgive them for they know not what they do"* (Luke 23:34).

That is why Hebrews 12 says that the blood of Jesus is crying much better things than the blood of Abel (v. 24). Abel's blood is crying, "God, avenge me. My brother has murdered me and taken away my life." (Genesis 4:10) Yet the blood of Jesus is crying, "Give mercy, forgive them, for they know not what they do." Mercy triumphs over judgment (James 2:13).

The Threshing Floor

I was discussing with a friend recently the fact that it is often difficult to see healing come to seasoned Christians, yet non-

Christians are often relatively easy to pray for and we see God heal them and do miracles. You can pray for fellow employees at work or you can pray for the man in the street; God will do all kinds of miraculous answers to prayer for people who don't know the Lord. But some dear old saint who has been serving the Lord for years will have nothing happen when you pray healing for him or her. Why? Perhaps there are issues needing forgiveness and repentance which God has repeatedly called for, yet through fear, pride, anger or pain, they remain unresolved. This can be a key for us. One answer to this question is revealed in 1 Corinthians 11. But remember, this is only one of the factors, so don't go on a guilt trip here.

> *For I received from the Lord what I also passed on to you: The Lord Jesus, on the night he was betrayed, took bread, and when he had given thanks, he broke it and said, "This is my body, which is for you; do this in remembrance of me."*

> *In the same way, after supper he took the cup, saying, "This cup is the new covenant in my blood; do this, whenever you drink it, in remembrance of me." For whenever you eat this bread and drink this cup, you proclaim the Lord's death until he comes.*

> *Therefore, whoever eats the bread or drinks the cup of the Lord in an unworthy manner will be guilty of sinning against the body and blood of the Lord. A man ought to examine himself before he eats of the bread and drinks of the cup. For anyone who eats and drinks without recognizing the body of the Lord eats and drinks **judgment** on himself.*

(vv. 23-29, emphasis mine)

I have read that passage for years thinking it was only referring to the communion elements. But it is not only referring to the broken body of our Lord Jesus Christ. It also refers to His body, the Church! We are His bride, and His body is precious to Him. It grieves Him deeply when we speak against the body of the Lord Jesus Christ by speaking against one another. Paul continues,

*That is why many among you are weak and sick, and a
number of you have fallen asleep. But if we judged ourselves,
we would not come under judgment.* (v. 30-31)

What a powerful word. If we will admit our own sins of judging
everybody and everything, and ask God to forgive us, we will not
come under judgment. But because many of us Christians are
judging and condemning 80 percent of the time, I believe the
Lord has taken us to the threshing floor. I believe we are in a do-
or-die season, a crisis time. Our lives will go one way or the other
on the threshing floor. It is the place of crisis.

John said, *"He will baptize you with the Holy Spirit and with
fire"* (Matthew 3:11). Well, I want you to know that His winnowing
fan is in His hand, and He will thoroughly purge His floor.

The Place of Grace

The Lord wants to knock this chaff off us and set us free, burning
the undesirable things up so that we will, with a pure heart, flow
in the grace, love and mercy of God.

You see, justice is good, and the world tries to live there. I thank
God for justice, for the police and the courts and the laws, but
there is a higher and a better place. There is a place where Satan
cannot follow you, the place of the grace of the Lord Jesus Christ.
This is what Christianity is all about. It is here that life and mercy
flow, for ourselves and others.

Do you know that when you live in grace, you are invincible
until God is finished with you? The enemy can't follow you there.
How can Satan follow you into a place of God's grace? There is
no grace for him. He is stuck with the law. But we can live in
grace and be absolutely dependent on the Holy Spirit's ability to
keep us.

Jesus is totally and absolutely victorious in all of these areas.
He completely defeated Satan. Jesus is God, who came as a man,
but as a man empowered by the Holy Spirit because He had the
Spirit without measure (John 3:34). He completely defeated Satan
and all of his hordes of hell single-handedly. Nothing has

24

changed. They are still defeated. Yet we give Satan power when we choose justice rather than mercy.

Somebody once told me that as a Christian I didn't have rights anymore. This is absolutely true. The only rights we have are to be completely forgiven, to go to heaven when we die, to be a love slave to the Lord Jesus Christ and to rely completely on Him for everything.

3

Set Free From the Fruits of Judgment

(Carol Arnott)

See to it that no one misses the grace of God and that no bitter root grows up to cause trouble and defile many.

(Hebrews 12:15)

How does this apply to our lives?

When I became a Christian I learned about forgiveness. So I forgave my mother, who had hurt me deeply, for everything and anything; yet I found that I still didn't love her. I went through it all again, only to find that I still didn't love her. So I did it again, and again and I still didn't love her. I thought, God, there must be something wrong. What is wrong with my forgiveness?

Judging Born Out of Hurt

My mom was the last of eight children; the sixth girl. The family was hoping for more boys to work the farm, so my mom wasn't even wanted. She was just another girl.

Since her parents often worked in the field, her sisters were expected to raise her. But kids being kids they were often very mean to her. They would rock her violently in her cradle. When she cried as a little toddler, they would lock her in a closet. You can imagine the wounds these events caused in her heart.

As a child growing up I didn't understand my mother's pain and rejection. I didn't know the depths of her hurts. I just had to deal with how she was to me. When kids do something wrong, when they are bad and really deserve a spanking, they know it. But when children are punished for things that they didn't do, they are keenly aware of the injustice. They may not rebel outwardly, but in their hearts they judge their parents as mean or unjust.

That's what happened to me. In my case I was too afraid to rebel outwardly because I would get severely spanked. My mother would take my dad's belt and whack me. Today it would be called abuse. I would be black and blue and have welts on my body, but the deeper marks were left on the inside. In my heart I hated her; inside I judged her and despised her.

When I became a Christian, I realized I had a lot of unforgiveness in my heart that needed to be released. I worked through all I could, but it didn't seem to change my feelings toward my mother. I thought, God, there is something wrong here. Over and over I tried, but my heart was not changed. It wasn't until I received some teaching from John and Paula Sandford about judgments rooted in bitterness that I gained more understanding.

The Scripture says to honor your father and your mother only if they are good Christians and if they do everything right. Oops. No, it doesn't say that, does it? Don't you wish? ... No, it says,

> *Honor your father and your mother, as the Lord your God has commanded you, so that you may live long and that it may go well with you in the land the Lord your God is giving you.* (Deuteronomy 5:16)

Conversely, in the areas in which you dishonor them, it will not go well with you. We do not judge them in every area, of course, but we judge and dishonor them in the areas where we have been hurt and neglected.

I thought, Well, God, I don't understand. I have forgiven her. What is going on? He said, "You have not honored her. You have sinned by dishonoring your mother." He began to show me that there were two sides to the issue. We need to forgive, yes, but we also need to repent of our own sin of judging. On one hand I needed to forgive her, so I did that. But on the other, I didn't honor her in my heart. I hated her. I judged her.

That was my sin, not hers. My reaction to her was sinful, yet I didn't see that. Satan, being a legalist, went to God and said,

"God, Carol has sinned here. She has not repented from this sin of judging her mother, so I have the legal right to bring the law of sowing and reaping into Carol's life."

Reaping What I Sowed

Have you ever kept a garden and planted a seed, of corn, for example? Consider a corn plant. How many seeds (kernels) do you get back? One? No, hundreds. Plant one and get hundreds, that is the law of increase. So, through my judgments of a domineering, controlling mother, I reaped a harvest through other domineering, controlling women in my life.

I would get controlled and manipulated, used and hurt by these women, and I could never see the problems coming. When they did come, I would think, God, what did I do to bring this on? Have I got a sign on my back that says, "Come on, control me? Come on, dominate me?"

Well, yes, I did have a sign. In the spirit realm I wore a sign because I judged my mother. The law of sowing and reaping was being enforced by the enemy.

Eventually I went to my mom. By this time she was a Christian, and I said, "Mom, I just received some teaching, and I realize that I have sinned against you. I have judged you. I have hated you in my heart and I really want to work things through."

She said, "Carol, I don't want to talk about it. I am too old. Too much has happened. I don't want you ever to mention this to me again."

I thought, Now what am I going to do?

God Does the Healing

The Lord said, "Carol, do you want to be healed?" I said, "Yes, Lord, I want to be healed."

He said, "Give me permission to dig in the garden of your heart. I don't want you to go rooting around, start navel-gazing or turning everything up and being worried and full of striving. Give Me

29

permission to bring up the issues where you have judged and which need to be dealt with." I said, "Okay. Lord, I give you permission."

Then I said a blanket prayer: "God, I realize that I have sinned by judging my mom and not honoring her. Lord, I forgive her for everything that she has ever done to me. She owes me nothing. I ask for Your forgiveness, and I give You permission to show me the areas that I need to put right."

That prayer initiated a trek of three and a half years of major dealing with issues. The Lord would bring up ten, sometimes fifteen instances of judgment a day – things that I had long forgotten about. I worked through situations I had not thought about since the day they happened.

I would pray, "Lord, I sinned by judging my mother. I forgive her for that incident. I did not honor her in it. I judged her and I hated her. Lord, I forgive her. Please, Lord, forgive me for the sin of judging my mother." I prayed without any big feeling in my heart; nothing emotional really seemed to happen.

I would see my mom maybe twice a week or more, and to the best of my ability, I would try to love her. I would tell her I loved her and give her a hug. I did the best I was able to do.

About three years into the process, I was visiting mom one day. When I was about to leave, I hugged her, told her I loved her, then said goodbye. But this time a surprising and wonderful love welled up in my heart for my mother. I knew I was healed. I knew that God had done a work in my heart.

You know what else? Not only did God heal me, but when I released my mom, it set her free too. She is so much better. She is so much freer and much more loving. My healing allowed God to do mighty works in her life even though she wasn't able to work through the issues herself because of her pain and lack of knowledge and application of Scripture.

Giving Satan Legal Rights

John and I have pastored two churches. Our first church was in Stratford. People would come to me and complain to me but never

30

to John. They felt neglected or rejected and would dump all their negativity on me. I would tell John how people were treating me, but he wouldn't or couldn't hear me.

If any of you have ever heard John speak about me, you know he absolutely adores me. He loves me, and I know that if anyone tried to hurt me, he would stand up for me. But when it came to the people in church, he seemed unable to.

I would go to him and tell him what was said, and sometimes he would say, "Oh, you are just jealous," or "You are overreacting again," or "That is not all that serious." I would be devastated. "God, what is wrong?" I asked.

Then, when we started the church in Toronto, guess what the people there did? They didn't go to John with their complaints; they came to me. I went to John, and he wouldn't stand up for me. He wouldn't even take my side or hear what they were saying. This was driving me to distraction.

Finally I cried out, "God, what on earth is going on? What am I reaping here?" And the Lord said, "What about your father?" I was shocked. "My father? My father is wonderful. I love my father. My father is a sweetheart. He is a gentleman. He is a loving and kind man. I have no judgments against my father."

The Lord said, "Oh yes, you do." I said, "I do? What judgments?" He said, "You judged your father because he did not protect you from your mother."

Those judgments gave the enemy legal rights that resulted in the primary man in my life, John, not being able to protect me from "mother" church. The church then was able to dump all her rubbish on me. John was not able to stand up for me. The laws of judging, and of sowing and reaping, gave the enemy what he needed.

I thought, Wow, Lord, could that be possible? I was still reasonably new to this kind of teaching. It sounded so strange. So I went to a girlfriend and said, "I think this is what the Lord has been telling me. I want to confess it to you. I am not going to tell John.

"I am just going to forgive my father for not standing up for me and for not protecting me against my mother's wrath. I am going to release and forgive him, and then I am going to forgive John for not standing up for me, for not protecting me from the people in the church. I am going to ask the Lord to forgive me for judging my father and John."

I asked the Lord to put the cross of Jesus between my heart and the law of sowing and reaping, and I left it all there.

Two months later there was another incident. A lady came to me and dumped all her rubbish on me. I went to John and immediately he said, "We are going to call her into the office." He called her in, stood up for me and dealt with the situation. It was amazing. He has been the same way ever since.

My judgments had given Satan legal right to hold John in bondage and prevent him from being my protector.

If there are areas in your life where repetitive, negative things keep happening; if there are areas where you are unable to love someone as you should; look back and say, "Holy Spirit, will you show me? Will you reveal it to me if have I judged a primary person in my life? Have I dishonored him or her?"

You may not be in touch with your anger, hurt and emotions. You may have no recollection of ever judging anyone, but if repetitive, negative fruit is in your life, there is usually a judgment rooted in bitterness, anger or hurt, that is allowing the enemy access. Keep in mind that it will not be in every area of your life, but it will be in the areas where you have been hurt and wounded.

Set Free

The Lord has come to set the captives free, to heal the brokenhearted, and to open the prison doors (Isaiah 61:1). He has come to do that, not only for me, but for all of us.

I believe the enemy has held us in bondage and kept much of the body of Christ in darkness when the Lord has a way of release and forgiveness available. Satan tries to keep this truth hidden from the body of Christ. The Bible says, *"My people are destroyed from lack of knowledge"* (Hosea 4:6).

In my own life this truth has meant more to me than a million dollars ever could. It has meant healing and freedom. God has set me free. It is so gloriously liberating.

4

It's Time to Forgive

(John Arnott)

Now we can understand what the scripture means when it says, *"I will give you the keys to the kingdom of heaven; whatever you bind on earth will be bound in heaven, and whatever you loose on earth will be loosed in heaven"* (Matthew 16:19).

It is time to take these keys away from the enemy by recognizing where we have these issues, these IOUs*, these outstanding judgments that are deeply rooted in pain and bitterness. We need to uncover the areas where we are calling out for God's justice, and deal with them through forgiveness and repentance. Holding on to hurts and judgments is a luxury you and I can't afford. It is like giving Satan a key to your house.

Loosing Others Through Forgiveness

We have been given a treasure. When we gave our lives to Jesus, we went from nothing to everything. We have been forgiven a huge debt of sin, and God is saying now, "The least you can do is to forgive your fellow servants, your parents, your brothers."

I know of women whose brothers literally tortured them as they were growing up. Things may have happened to you that have caused you to hate men, or to hate women.

When my first marriage broke up, I made a vow in my heart that no woman would ever hurt me like that again. It took me quite a while, with Carol's help, to break down that vow. Carol, of course, penetrated my defenses, and thank God she did. I was able to be healed of bitter rooted judgments and see mercy triumph over judgment (James 2:13).

---

* Notes of an owed debt – 'I owe you".

33

Often the tragedies of life are so serious and so severe that we can't imagine ourselves letting go of them, especially with one simple prayer. Sometimes the wound is too fresh, and we need more time.

One of the reasons why Paul the apostle had such an outstanding conversion was because a man named Stephen who they were stoning to death, understood this principle and cried out, *"Lord, do not hold this sin against them"* (Acts 7:60).

Perhaps his eyes caught the eyes of young Saul of Tarsus at that moment. Because Stephen forgave, there was no binding in the heavens, no surrendering of keys and rights to the enemy so he would be able legally to hold that young man, Saul. God later powerfully intervened, and Saul had a dramatic conversion. Today we know him as Paul, the apostle to the Gentiles.

We are to give others a gift they don't deserve when there is no question that we have been sinned against, hurt and violated by them. Yes, an outstanding debt exists. They owe us, but we can give them an undeserved gift—our forgiveness. We can step into the mercy of God and say, "I want mercy to triumph over justice." This is what God is asking for.

The grace of the Lord Jesus Christ is more than enough for me. I am going to give a gift of forgiveness to those who have hurt me and sinned against me. I am going to give them a gift they don't deserve – my forgiveness – just as my heavenly Father has given me a gift that I don't deserve – His forgiveness. I want mercy for me, not the justice I deserve. Therefore, I choose to forgive all others. It is the merciful who obtain mercy (Matthew 5:7).

Sometimes it takes a while, just as Carol said, to give the Holy Spirit permission to uncover the issues. But God wants to make us into free, happy and joy-filled people. We don't have the time or energy to keep a lid on all of the hurts, angers and fears that the enemy brings into our lives through the law of sowing and reaping.

Remember, Satan will move through legal rights. We need to give up our rights, surrendering and saying, "Lord, I want to do things Your way." We can be like Jesus and Stephen who said, "Lay not this sin to their charge." Let's tell God, "I forgive them, and I ask You to forgive me for judging them in bitterness and hurt, and for demanding that something be done about it."

Keep in mind that I am not talking about situations where loving or pastoral correction needs to be brought. I am talking about issues that are poisoning your heart, areas where you are literally giving Satan access to your life, enabling him to come in and bring destruction any time he chooses.

There is a place of quiet rest near the heart of God. There is a place under the shadow of the Almighty. There is a place at the cross of Jesus Christ where mercy triumphs over judgment and you can come into the glorious liberty of the sons of God. It is the place of grace and mercy.

I am not going to put a gun to your head and say you have to forgive. That doesn't work. We have all been told things like, "Well, I don't care what they did. If you are a Christian, you have to forgive!" No, you don't have to forgive. You can hold onto it if you like, but understand the dynamics.

You are entitled to justice, but then you will also reap what you have sown. You, too, will receive the justice you deserve instead of mercy. When I understood that, I knew what Jesus meant when he said, *"Blessed are the merciful: for they shall obtain mercy"* (Matthew 5:7).

Let Forgiveness Flow

I believe the word of the Lord has penetrated your heart like a sword, and the Holy Spirit has you at the threshing floor where He wants to knock some of this chaff off your life. Are there a few people you need to forgive?

Let me lead you in a prayer. Please don't strive. You may be saying, "Well, I will say the words, but I don't really mean them." It's okay, as long as in your heart you are saying, "Lord, help me to work through this. Make me willing to be willing." God honors that. Also, we are going to ask God to forgive us for the sin of judging others and ask Him to remind us graciously when we lapse into thinking negatively again.

Let's bless and curse not, and give undeserved gifts to people so we can be vessels of honor and mercy. Become a new wineskin that will hold the new wine and the oil of the Holy Spirit, enabling you to walk in freedom and love.

But before I lead in that prayer, let's take a moment and wait upon God. Be bathed in the presence of the Holy Spirit. Invite Him to come upon you afresh. Don't strive to do this in religious strength or out of your own willpower. I want you to know, that without the Holy Spirit's enabling, you won't be able to proceed. Some of the crimes against you are just too extreme.

Some of you have been so abused. The circumstances you have gone through and the things that have happened to you were never, never the Father's heart. They were born from sin loosed in the world and from your own wrong choices, as well as other people who have hurt you. God is not responsible for the sins of man.

We can defeat the devil. We can make sure that the sins of the fathers are not passed on to the children to the third and fourth generation. For if you don't deal with your legalistic judgments, and step into grace and mercy, the Bible says that the problems are passed on to your children (Exodus 20:5). The master legalist, Satan, will see to it.

Let's pray together.

> We worship You, Father. We come and acknowledge our need. We ask for the presence of the Holy Spirit to come and help us. We choose mercy over judgment. We want to give gifts of forgiveness to those who hurt us and those who don't deserve it. We want to defeat the enemy and take away his legal rights to harm us.

> Father, I choose to forgive the ones who have hurt me so deeply and sinned against me. I forgive my mother. I forgive my father. I forgive my brothers. I forgive my sisters. I forgive my husband. I forgive my wife. I forgive my employers and my pastors and my friends and everyone who has sinned against me. I give them the gift of unconditional forgiveness, with no strings attached. They owe me nothing. I trust God to turn it for good (Romans 8:28).

> Lord, I also forgive myself for my own failures and

mistakes. I let go of it all.

Lord, now I want to confess my sins. I have judged these whom I have mentioned in bitterness and anger. I want to be free. Forgive me, Father, for dishonoring my parents, my pastor, my friends. Forgive me for becoming part of the problem rather than part of the solution. It was my own pride that was demanding justice.

Lord, I want to be free. I want to break the hold of the enemy in my life. I put the cross of Jesus Christ between my heart and everything I was due to reap from the law of sowing and reaping. I give you permission, Holy Spirit, to bring up whatever specific issues you want to bring up so that I can forgive specifically and repent specifically, because I do choose mercy over judgment.

I tear up all these IOUs and throw them at the foot of the cross. I say that Your grace is sufficient for me. Whatever I loose on earth is loosed in heaven, and I loose it all into your capable hands. I now give You Lord permission to move powerfully in my life. In Jesus' name. Amen.

Now, let me pray a prayer of authority and declaration over you:

Father, I take away the rights of the enemy over the lives of these people. Satan, I break your generational hold over God's people. I command you to loose them and let them go in the mighty name of Jesus Christ, God's holy Son. Free them, by the blood of Jesus that has never lost its power. I free you, woman of God. I free you, man of God. I free you, child of God. Mercy now triumphs over judgment.

I break off you all of those controlling fears, controlling anger, rejection and every hold of the enemy, in the name of Jesus Christ. I free you to rise to your full potential in Jesus Christ, your Savior and Lord. The Lion of the tribe of Judah has triumphed over all the power of the enemy. We put the enemy under our feet and step up into the grace of God. In Jesus' mighty and powerful name. Amen.

And forgive us our debts, as we have also forgiven our debtors (Matthew 6:12).

If you have enjoyed this book and would like to help us to send a copy of it and many other titles to needy pastors in the **Third World**, please write for further information or send your gift to:

Sovereign World Trust, P.O. Box 777, Tonbridge, Kent TN11 0ZS, United Kingdom

or to the **'Sovereign World'** distributor in your country.

You may contact the author by writing to:

Toronto Airport Christian Fellowship
272 Attwell Drive,
Toronto, ON,
CANADA, M9W 6M3

Phone no: 416-674-8463
Fax no: 416-674-8465
email: ja@tacf.org